The Satisfactory Nothing of Girls

poems by

Emily Bowles

Finishing Line Press
Georgetown, Kentucky

The Satisfactory Nothing of Girls

Copyright © 2021 by Emily Bowles
ISBN 978-1-64662-600-7 First Edition
All rights reserved under International and Pan-American Copyright Conventions. No part of this book may be reproduced in any manner whatsoever without written permission from the publisher, except in the case of brief quotations embodied in critical articles and reviews.

ACKNOWLEDGMENTS

Unless otherwise noted, direct quotations refer to Virginia Woolf's novel The Voyage Out (1915).
"Cucumbering a Sunbeam" was published online by Brainmill Press (Summer 2020) and received a Pushcart Prize nomination.

Publisher: Leah Huete de Maines
Editor: Christen Kincaid
Cover Art: Emily Bowles
Author Photo: Aurora Smith
Cover Design: Elizabeth Maines McCleavy

Order online: www.finishinglinepress.com
also available on amazon.com

Author inquiries and mail orders:
Finishing Line Press
PO Box 1626
Georgetown, Kentucky 40324
USA

Table of Contents

A letter to Rachel Vinrace 1

I. BOUGHT

I Deny You Her (Beauty) 5
Nicole Kidman's Nose 6
Her Words Fall Flat 8
Roomsical Women 9
What Clarissa Seas 10

II. BOUND

You Are Not / Beautiful 13
Prismprisons 14
Goat on the Green 16
Tulips 17
Richards 18

III. BURIED

Your Breath During Yoga Class 21
Childish Women 22
Cucumbering a Sunbeam 23
Each to Each 26
The Way We Treat Flowers 27
How We Hold on to Brooms 29

For Melissa, who helped me re-remember my Dalloway, and for Aurora, always

She glanced at Rachel again. Yes! how clear it was that she would be vacillating, emotional, and when you said something to her, it would make no more lasting impression than the stroke of a stick upon the water. There was nothing to take hold of in girls—nothing hard, permanent, satisfactory.
—Virginia Woolf, *The Voyage Out*

A Letter to Rachel Vinrace

Dear Miss Vinrace—or may I presume, as I have watched you die three times now, to call you by your first name? Please, Rachel, think it not a presumption, for you will come to find that I have developed a strange affection for you, more so than other not-favorite characters in favorite authors works, for to be fair, you are not Clarissa, and that is why, I think at nearly twice your age, I still see myself as you at 24.

I am, as you were to Helen, an unlasting impression, the mark of a stick on the water, as transitory as I am unintelligible and worse, common. How many ripples like me, mine, appear on the surface, a moment of eddying or of change in depth, color, movement and are forgotten before they've (we've, I've) even had a chance to be seen, sensed?

For you, a ship on the Amazon; for me, a shipment from amazon.

Object lessons we learn without being learned ourselves, without mattering despite the rhetoric penetrating us "now more than ever" we need—something no one can give us, nothing. Unfilled, unfilling, unfulfilling.

Your ship sailed, my shipment arrived, and you and I both release stories sea seeing, unseen, like flower petals, blown out blooms not without cost beyond what Clarissa could pay.

Her husband.

Flattening, flattering, knowing nothing of ourselves (mine) we write of others, pretend or presume and leave.

I write to and through you, for you, because you have weathered [nothing] a hundred years of your own satisfactory nothing, my own unsatisfactory nothing, no more lasting, we.

Reading you now, cloistered because of COVID-19, I am as if on a ship and in that relentless space you knew so well, a space in which your small world felt like everything and nothing at once. We have our parallels, and each page of your story repeats itself yet reminds me even when we repeat ourselves (so many times since March 13 have I done so, repeated without revising the wrong parts of my story, debts and divorces from words, meanings, men, anxieties, devices). I am your story as I read it, my own when I don't, and so I read you again, in need, in desperation, as we all are, as no one knows.

I should be Clarissa by now.

I cannot buy flowers now.

Stores are closed, and my budget does not account for such things. I can, however, bind up what I take from the world around me—tulips, wildflowers—and create not a garland but instead a deadness of my own, a graveyard of pressed flowers in the library books I have heavily stacked up since their doors shut, each a souvenir of an outside where the world continues, despite_____this abrupt beginending.

xoxoxo your would-be Goat

I. Bought

Mrs Dalloway said she would buy the flowers herself.
　—Virginia Woolf, *Mrs. Dalloway*

I Deny You Her (Beauty)

Where "Beauty goes unregarded—eccentricity must pay the penalty,"
and with a mind like a "wound exposed," a face turns "weak":

    denied beauty

yet it is in the hesitation, the unspeaking
that she becomes
"more than normal[]"

incompetent or just
incomprehensibly
in bodied.

I deny you her
beauty
because

she is wounded, weak—not
normal,   or too
normal   (we can be both) to
survive.

Nicole Kidman's Nose

> *Imagine the great brilliance of Virginia Woolf to be turned into this absolutely maimed fool with a really ugly nose.*
> —Patricia Cohen, "The Nose Was the Final Straw"

1.
I have her nose,
the prosthetic one
layered on top to create
a fiction of ugliness,
a fact I wear without Art.

2.
When I run, I feel
beautiful   strong
ugly   weak
stride by stride, side by side
dichotomies make me sprint
when I should tread cautiously,
a river bug flies into my ear
Emily Dickinson-style
my face finds me
in a moving reflection,
a windowpane
a window pain
plain Jane with a large nose.

3.
When God was giving out Noses,
I thought he said Roses,
so I asked for a big red one.

4.
Laugh, don't laugh, no-
body who are you,
looking at me as intently as I am
looking at these not-roses along the river?

5.
I broke it
myself, naturally, when the wind made my car door
swingswing
hit me hard, arms full of groceries,
buying not-the-flowers my/her-
self, and I didn't ask for it
[help, I mean], the kind of Nose
satirists love, the kind of Nose
that makes me a Commonplace snorer,
each breath an effort too loud, too hurting.

6.
I will rewatch it, rewind it.

7.
The disappointing part,
that's the story of hers most mine.

Her Words Fall Flat

You composed her face.

Words fall flat, sometimes,
at parties and in those awkward exchanges,
emails and texts all surface, smaller than the palm
of your hand, which is all Clarissa saw
she said, a lie:

"you see round...I only see there,"
the flat palm,
back of the hand Women Like Us have felt the flattening.

She flatters him / He flattens her.

Fallen
        for Rachel,
        with Rachel,
        Rachel.
Flatten
      for a moment of relief,

not unlike the Other Woman whose face "testified to flatness within"
perhaps written by such a palm. Be tractable; compose it,
your flat face.

Roomsical Women

Rooms—I call you—Virginia, from this space of shut in-ness,
where I fold into myself a story more miniscule than the bit of ivory,
where I fold sheets that tell a story more violent than the bit of ivory,
a piano should be here, or a war, something with notes or of note, not
[this absence of self from life and life from self, infinitely largesmall].

What Clarissa Seas

Violence at midlife
       I mean,
violets at midlife
middling
       I mean,
mid-ocean:

"What I find so tiresome about the sea is that there are no flowers in it. Imagine fields of hollyhocks and violets in mid-ocean!"

What Clarissa seas
              I mean,
what Clarissa sees
is a Man larger than Life,
death defiantly
boring, tiresome
without flowers
without meaning.

II. Bound

*I will bind flowers in one garland and clasp them and present them—
Oh! to whom?*
    —Virginia Woolf, *The Waves*

You Are Not / Beautiful

"She walks in beauty" was the first
poem I learned line by line,

        and now I know it's
a line,

a line
no shorter than the lines for
bathroom stalls in bars

a line
no longer than the lines like
"a girl walked into a bar" jokes,

a line
that worked on Rachel Vinrace: "You're not beautiful, but
I like...
I like...
I like..."

Reader, she [would have] married him
...like I
did, like we do,
these men who make you feel like you're not beautiful, but
they'll settle for "your face,
your hair,
your eyes,"
        like
they're doing us a favor by settling,
        like
they're deserving of mermaids.

I like mermaids better than men too, I want to say,
I like to disappear into "a sea mist," that drowns out—disappearing
them, these un-
beauteous lines.

Prismprisons

1.

"The next few months passed away, as many years can pass away, without definite events, and yet, if suddenly disturbed, it would be seen that such months or years had a character unlike others" (read this/ write it Marching in/in March 2020).

It was Friday the thirteenth when we turned outside in, made the domestic the center rather than the margins, made screens the scenes and scenes about sanity/sanitizing.

2.

"The next few months passed away, as many years can pass away, without definite events, and yet, if suddenly disturbed, it would be seen that such months or years had a character unlike others" (*ibid* April, the cruelest month).

Marianne Moore called them days of prismatic color, the days when Adam was alone, and we are in them now, these days hyperpigmented by our screens, shedding blue light on what was not paradise, before Eve.

3.

"The next few months passed away, as many years can pass away, without definite events, and yet, if suddenly disturbed, it would be seen that such months or years had a character unlike others" (*ibid* May— MayDay!, they say in *The Handmaid's Tale*, domestic battlecrying).

Inside, nothing happens and everything too, outside, the same: infinitesimal smallness confounds itself with vastness. When I look at people through car windows, behind plexiglass at stores, I see their faces flatten into Faces, symbols, types (e.g., those who refuse and those who conform, categories that shift diurnally).

4.

"The next few months passed away, as many years can pass away, without definite events, and yet, if suddenly disturbed, it would be seen that such months or years had a character unlike others" (*ibid* June, my mother's 77th birthday, my father's 43rd father's day for/to/from me). I write on the edge of June.

"The next few months passed away, as many years can pass away, without definite events, and yet, if suddenly disturbed, it would be seen that such months or years had a character unlike others" (*ibid* July, my birthday and "patriotism...the last refuge...to which a scoundrel clings" and when *Hamilton* livestreams). I write knowing July, knowing August too.

"The next few months passed away, as many years can pass away, without definite events, and yet, if suddenly disturbed, it would be seen that such months or years had a character unlike others" (*ibid*, August, when I used to run a race that ended in a crowded tent of people eating cheesecurds, drinking beer). I write not knowing, anything except the ibidness of it all.

Goat on the Green

She "was heard to sigh," to say:
"Poor little goats," louder in the first draft,
edited to   [ambiguity]
suggest what "depends upon goats," as a father
sharply says.

It is   or not
          sustainable:
this chomping at the bit,
this chewing on the green,
dandelions overgrowing
riotous, righteous
when economy and ecology
converge, covid-ingly,
labor lost, the groundskeepers
cheaper than
less grand fundable than
the Goats
ghosts, Virginia, Vita-
ly insisting on growth.

Tulips

You are [a] budding twolip.

He speaks of numbered streaks,
petal pedaling a story not yours.

I mean—a tulip and two bulbs:
"the firm red head and pale shaft,"
its "delicate green-tinted sap" in Winterson.

Our stories are numbered,
plucked one by one away for love,

lips locked, losing speaks.

Richards

How many Richards are Dicks, I wonder,
Dalloway, Gilmore, Joni Mitchell's song?

Essentialized, trivialized, bitches
to Savage, Johnson, preaching on hind legs.

Her second husband was one, a Richard,
Richard the second lesser in Shakespeare.

I have only used the word with humor,
hatred, for them, the men with different names.

Clarissa read Clarissa, Richardson,
and Austen was my grandmother's last name.

Her Richard was an Austen, her Austen
ending: an old man withered in a Bath.

I read them without living, loving my
own damaged Dalloway, shelved on my own.

III. Buried

All women together ought to let flowers fall upon the tomb of Aphra Behn, for it was she who earned them the right to speak their minds.
—Virginia Woolf, *A Room of One's Own*

Your Breath during Yoga Class

Death is like a yoga class, I think as I move through postures alone on
    my mat,
staring out a window at Life, at bodies separately sweating a river's
    distance from me:
we are thin, tired—and yet, Terence thought before she died that
    Rachel "was
the same as she had always been." He measures her breaths when he
    holds his, holds her.

The words are not so different from the words I hear, cueing me
(tone-deaf teachers who didn't know we'd be here #aparttogether):

perfectly
happy
peace
peace
move
speak
ease

"he held his breath"   "she was still breathing"
please hold your breath   while I am breathing
                                                  still,
                                                  until
"it was nothing; it was to cease to breathe," collectively our ending,
enduring.

Childish Women

She thinks us childish, women drowning drafts—
better, perhaps, to burn them like Amy.

He thinks it childish, that we drown in drafts,
now choicelessly paperless, ghosts of white pages.

Your childless woman is drowning drafts
of a marriage, a martyring, a mourning.

We are childish women, drowning drafts,
simple stories or complex, sticks on the water.

I am [not] childless, Margaret, drown my drafts:
paper bodies less[er] than your Blazing Worlds.[1]

I am childless, drowning my drafts
terrified when they come back, gaping for breath.

We are childless women, drowning [drafts],
unrevisability of petals on the water, and stones.

Your childish woman is drowning, daft
is draft without raft, nothing to hold onto.

That childless woman downing drafts,
she must have before pretending to birth—hares?[2]

She knew us childish, childless, drowned in drafts
of the wrong bodies, paper rock scissors surfacing.

---

[1] In her Sociable Letters, Margaret Cavendish described her drafts as paper bodies.

[2] During the eighteenth century, Mary Toft and her husband became tabloid celebrities of sorts when she confounded the medical community by giving birth to rabbits.

Cucumbering a Sunbeam

> *What a vision of loneliness and riot the thought of Margaret Cavendish brings to mind! as if some giant cucumber had spread itself over all the roses and carnations in the garden and choked them to death.*
> —Virginia Woolf, *A Room of One's Own*

For most people, Margaret Cavendish is a footnote[1] in literary history. For most people, cucumbers are not fruit or flower because they are green.

2.

She terrified Woolf—raging voices, staged in volumes of a length only the
Uneditable Elite might afford to print, her "paper bodies," she called them.

3.

Her husband's body had produced more ephemeral works, and a treatise on
horseback riding, as well as two daughters, both older than the Duchess.

---

[1]*Seventeenth-century writer Margaret Cavendish was of ambiguous origins before her marriage to the slightly foppish William Cavendish, Duke of Newcastle, whose daughters from his previous marriage bettered their father as elegant writers of manuscript prose and poetry. Margaret self-published wide-ranging books on philosophy, science, and more, while also writing seemingly impossible-to-perform plays, a utopian novel that explored many of her scientific theories, and a wild autobiography.*

[Footnote to this footnote: like Woolf, I have feelings for her that inflect my version of her Story, as has had Every Historian Who Has Ever Pretended Objectivity, for Cavendish beginning perhaps with Pepys and somewhat later Ballard but extending indefinitely.]

4.

I've been that woman, the same age as a man's daughter by his first wife, and
like Mad Madge, I relish in cucumbers as much as others like cake.

5.

They wrote for their father, for their coterie closet drama, coveting ambition,
writing of cake when surely their servants had their hands in that batter.

6.

We do not pick our mothers, although we try to write and rewrite them. They
revered one, ridiculed the other, and each became one, hating what was other.

7.

Margaret was accustomed to that misogyny or would soon be. Her desires were limit-
less, cosmic, a cucumber overgrowing its plot, her novels overgrowing their plots.

8.

She had stood before the Royal Society, spoke out before that audience of satirzable
pseudo-scientific Men, Pepys' pen ready to render her as the Object of their satire.

9.

Swift wrote not of Margaret but of the men who were "extracting sunbeams out of cucumbers."
He made light of their science, mad enough, unstable in a stable with Gulliver, eating apples.

10.

There are no roses, no carnations that can survive a lack of light like this, and so I kill
the plants in my apartment, eat a cucumber, imagine that sunbeam— for, from her.

Each to Each

Terence is not Prufrock,
still he makes her a mermaid;
she thinks she's made herself one.

I make mermaid tail blankets,
magically impractical, never for myself,
knit and purl only, easy, rhythmic stitches.

Handmade tails, *Handmaid Tales*,
the happy ending may be a death by drowning,
depending on Hans Christian Anderson or Disney.

"If we stood on a rock together,"
he said, and she said *apart together
apart together*, a refrain of COVID-19.

Who buys it, this narrative, this crashing
of wave against rock, of needle against yarn,
of mermaid against man, "sea heaving beneath?"

The Way We Treat Flowers

           1.

I ran today along a weedy path
up down up down up down up down
the same hill, different each time
when weeds gripped, grabbed
whipt me, cruelly, as if I had done
some Thing wrong, and so I did:
grabbed a tulip from a pedestal,
tucked it in my waistband, ran away.

           2.

Imlac would never_____
count a tulip that way.

           3.

Winterson, would, though,
and in rejecting, refusing Dr.
Johnson, I choose a crasser
story, or a kinder one, impossible
to say which is right, or true
(Johnson asked that, said it too).

           4.

Perhaps You gather
                [I gather flowers every day]
     [I gather you]
flowers
Yourself, and You understand
these are and are not for
Clarissa.

5.

One Clarissa died.

6.

Another Clarissa, the one I am
writing, bought flowers and
watched me (or Rachel)
watched you (or Septimus)
die in a whimpering whorl,
petals like Pound's bough.

How We Hold onto Brooms

1.

"How we perished," Woolf quoted Cowper elsewhere, but his letters bore [our] heroine, Rachel Vinrace, who only sees in them remnants of a bloom deader than her.

2.

How can a flower called a broom be anything but
tediously domestic,
suffocatingly domestic,
sweeping away any chance we have at
life outside of a circumscribed room?

3.

How we long for our mothers' gardens, like Walker's, like a fertile earth that eludes us, or me at least without even the sappiest saplingest baby of a green thumb.

4.

How much depends not
on a red wheelbarrow but
on a broom
on a room
on a bloom.

5.

How foolish
how futile
how cheerful
how chosen
the objects that hold our memories,
the objects that hold our mothers.

Emily Bowles received a PhD in English and Certificate in Women's Studies from Emory University in 2004. In her first chapbook, *His Journal, My Stella* (Finishing Line Press, 2018), she explores her experiences of gendered and sexual silencing in graduate school through the story of the subject of her thesis, Jonathan Swift. She has received the Wisconsin Fellowship of Poets' Triad Award, a Pushcart Prize nomination, and an artist residency with the Appleton Public Library. She serves on the Board of Directors of The Mill: A Place for Writers, has been a featured reader for Poetry Unlocked, and volunteers with Harbor House Domestic Abuse Services. Her work is available online at https://emilybowles1600.wixsite.com/mysite

www.ingramcontent.com/pod-product-compliance
Lightning Source LLC
LaVergne TN
LVHW041509070426
835507LV00012B/1442